1¢ or 10¢

Fold on dotted lines

Clear tape

Bend up

Bend up

Tape

Bend ailerons up

Side view

American Robin

Turdus migratorius

Famous in song, story, and legend, the Am[erican]
Robin is the mythical harbinger of spring [in]
North America. Its European namesake is [much]
smaller. The robin is a thrush, and is easily
recognized by its charcoal back and wing[s and]
russet-colored breast.

This early bird may often be seen in the cl[assic]
pose of pulling an earthworm from the la[wn. The]
eggs from a robin are so beautiful that th[ere is a]
color named robin's egg blue.

1¢ or 10¢

Fold on dotted lines

Clear tape

Bend up

Bend up

Tape

Bend ailerons up

Side view

Baltimore Oriole

Icterus galbula

Like the city, this bird is named for Lord Baltimore of old, whose coat of arms was orange and black. The sweet song of the Baltimore Oriole heralds springtime across the eastern United States. The Midwestern Northern Oriole is so similar that only geneticists can tell them apart!

Baltimore Orioles prefer less-dense forests, where they eat insects and berries, and the females make beautiful hanging nests. They like dark fruit and will ignore ripe fruit of lighter colors.

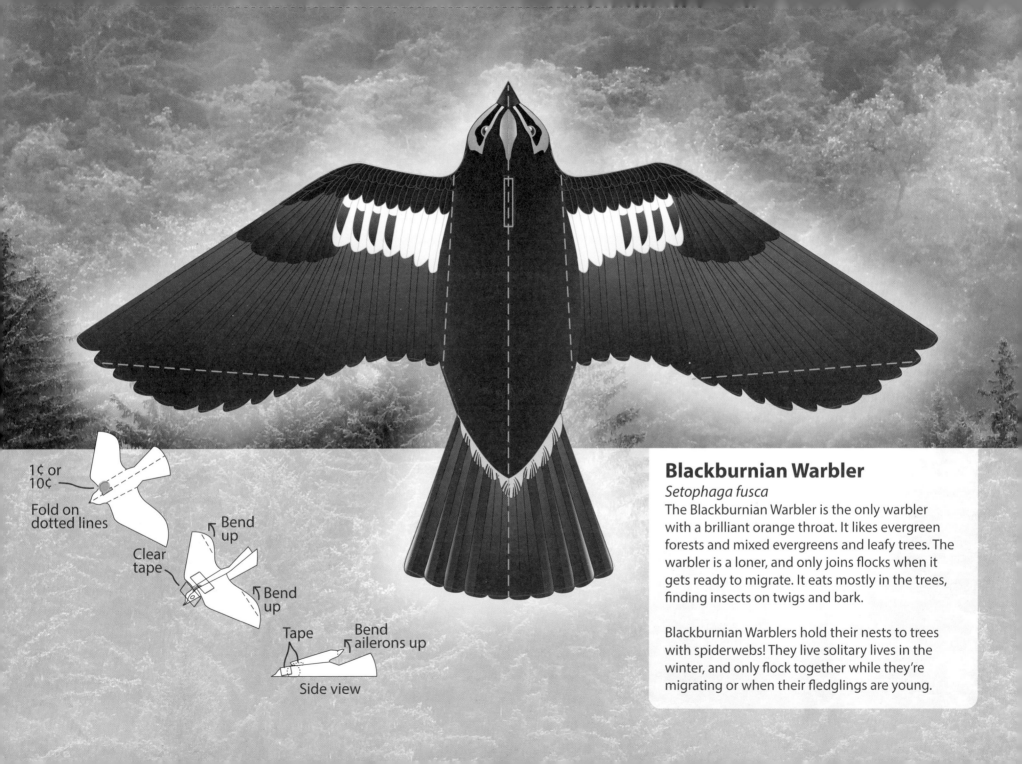

1¢ or
10¢

Fold on
dotted lines

Clear
tape

Bend
up

Bend
up

Tape

Bend
ailerons up

Side view

Blackburnian Warbler
Setophaga fusca

The Blackburnian Warbler is the only warbler with a brilliant orange throat. It likes evergreen forests and mixed evergreens and leafy trees. The warbler is a loner, and only joins flocks when it gets ready to migrate. It eats mostly in the trees, finding insects on twigs and bark.

Blackburnian Warblers hold their nests to trees with spiderwebs! They live solitary lives in the winter, and only flock together while they're migrating or when their fledglings are young.

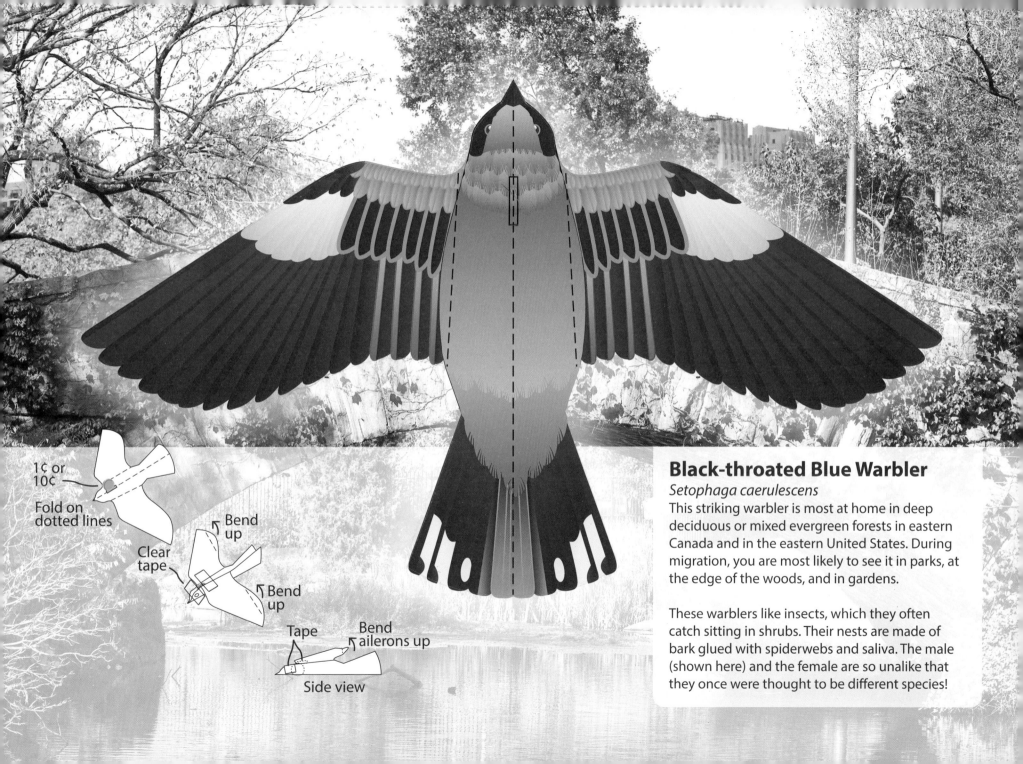

1¢ or 10¢

Fold on dotted lines

Clear tape

Bend up

Bend up

Tape

Bend ailerons up

Side view

Black-throated Blue Warbler
Setophaga caerulescens
This striking warbler is most at home in deep deciduous or mixed evergreen forests in eastern Canada and in the eastern United States. During migration, you are most likely to see it in parks, at the edge of the woods, and in gardens.

These warblers like insects, which they often catch sitting in shrubs. Their nests are made of bark glued with spiderwebs and saliva. The male (shown here) and the female are so unalike that they once were thought to be different species!

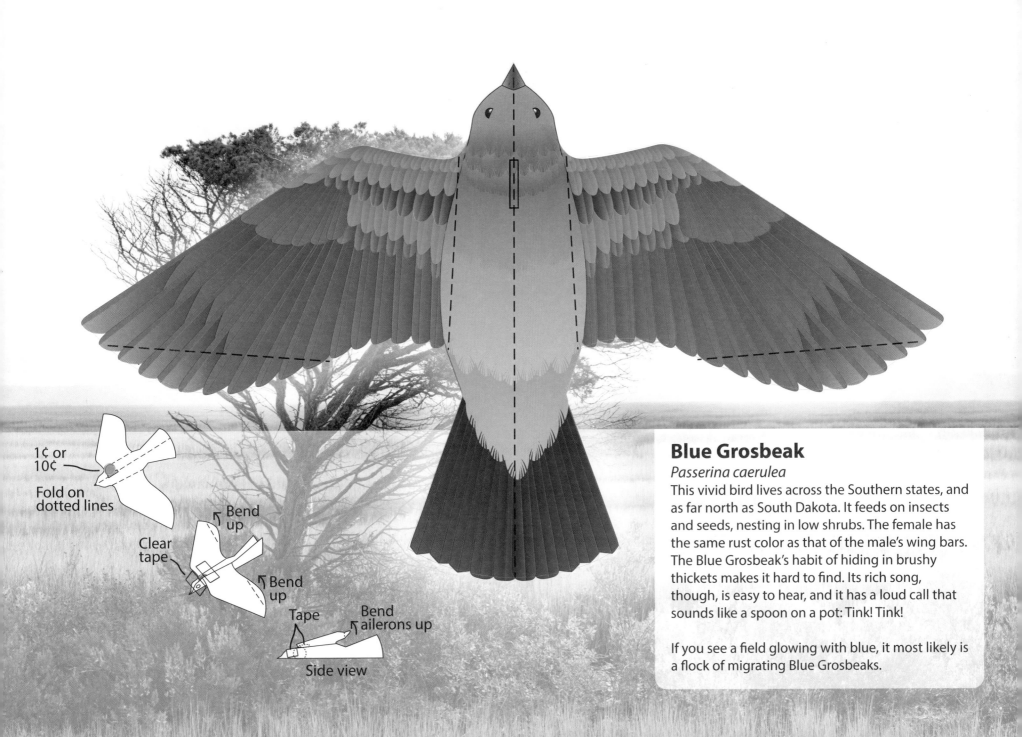

1¢ or 10¢

Fold on dotted lines

Clear tape

Bend up

Bend up

Tape

Bend ailerons up

Side view

Blue Grosbeak

Passerina caerulea

This vivid bird lives across the Southern states, and as far north as South Dakota. It feeds on insects and seeds, nesting in low shrubs. The female has the same rust color as that of the male's wing bars. The Blue Grosbeak's habit of hiding in brushy thickets makes it hard to find. Its rich song, though, is easy to hear, and it has a loud call that sounds like a spoon on a pot: Tink! Tink!

If you see a field glowing with blue, it most likely is a flock of migrating Blue Grosbeaks.

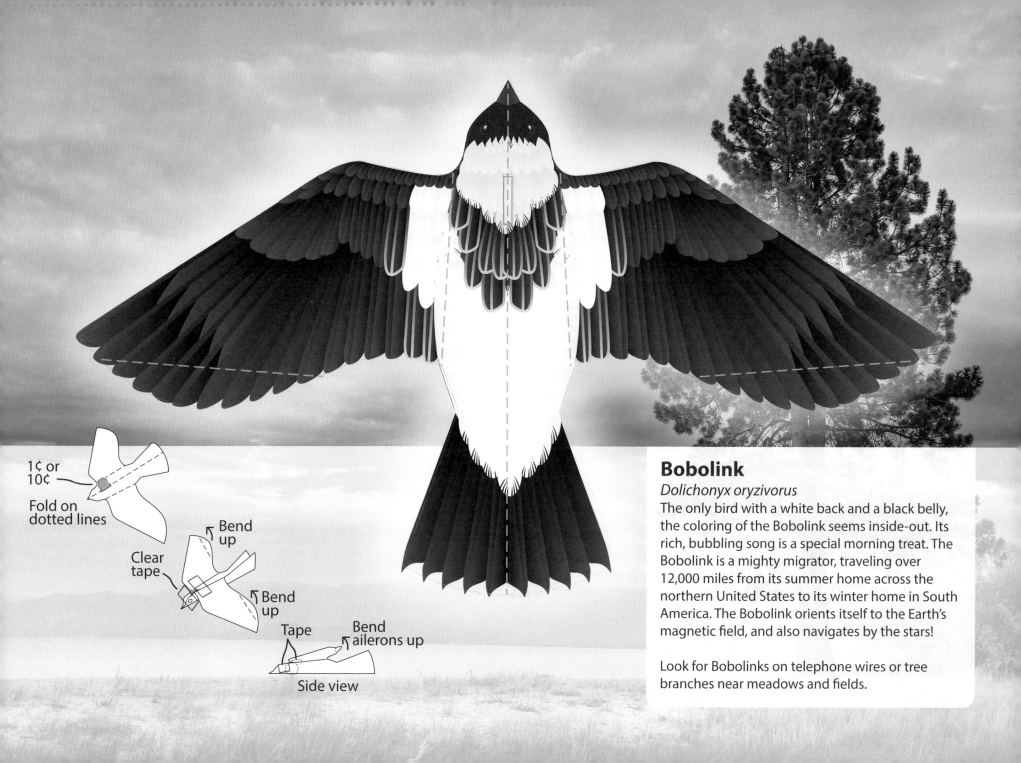

1¢ or 10¢

Fold on dotted lines

Clear tape

Bend up

Bend up

Tape

Bend ailerons up

Side view

Bobolink

Dolichonyx oryzivorus

The only bird with a white back and a black belly, the coloring of the Bobolink seems inside-out. Its rich, bubbling song is a special morning treat. The Bobolink is a mighty migrator, traveling over 12,000 miles from its summer home across the northern United States to its winter home in South America. The Bobolink orients itself to the Earth's magnetic field, and also navigates by the stars!

Look for Bobolinks on telephone wires or tree branches near meadows and fields.

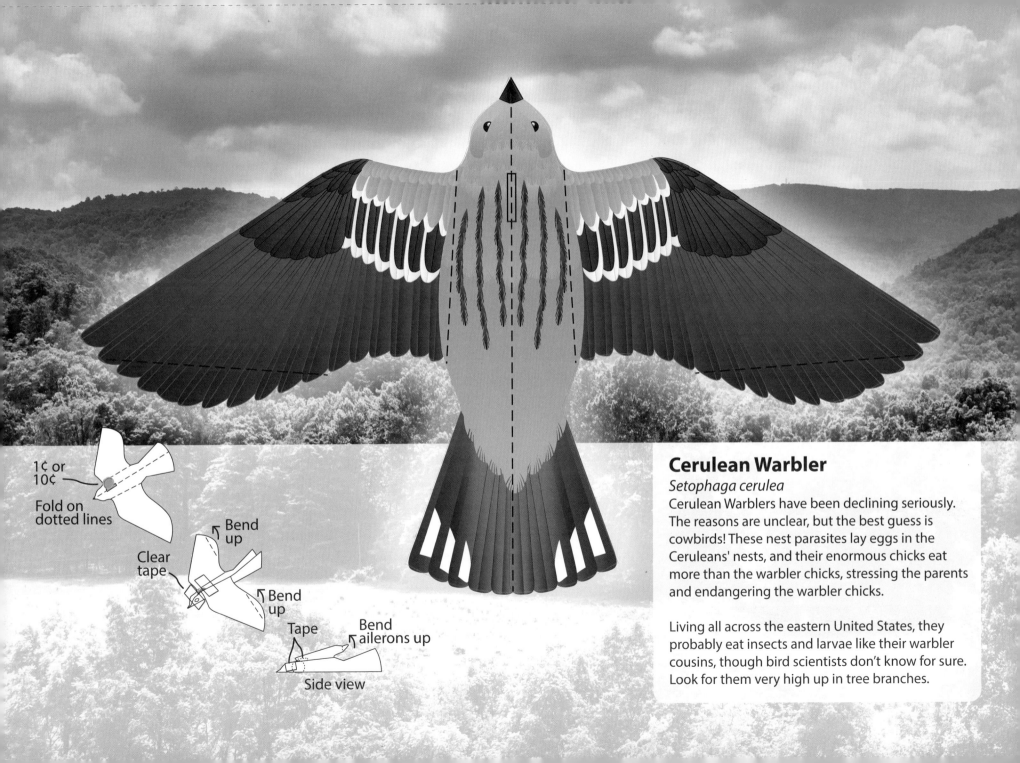

1¢ or 10¢

Fold on dotted lines

Clear tape

Bend up

Bend up

Tape

Bend ailerons up

Side view

Cerulean Warbler
Setophaga cerulea

Cerulean Warblers have been declining seriously. The reasons are unclear, but the best guess is cowbirds! These nest parasites lay eggs in the Ceruleans' nests, and their enormous chicks eat more than the warbler chicks, stressing the parents and endangering the warbler chicks.

Living all across the eastern United States, they probably eat insects and larvae like their warbler cousins, though bird scientists don't know for sure. Look for them very high up in tree branches.

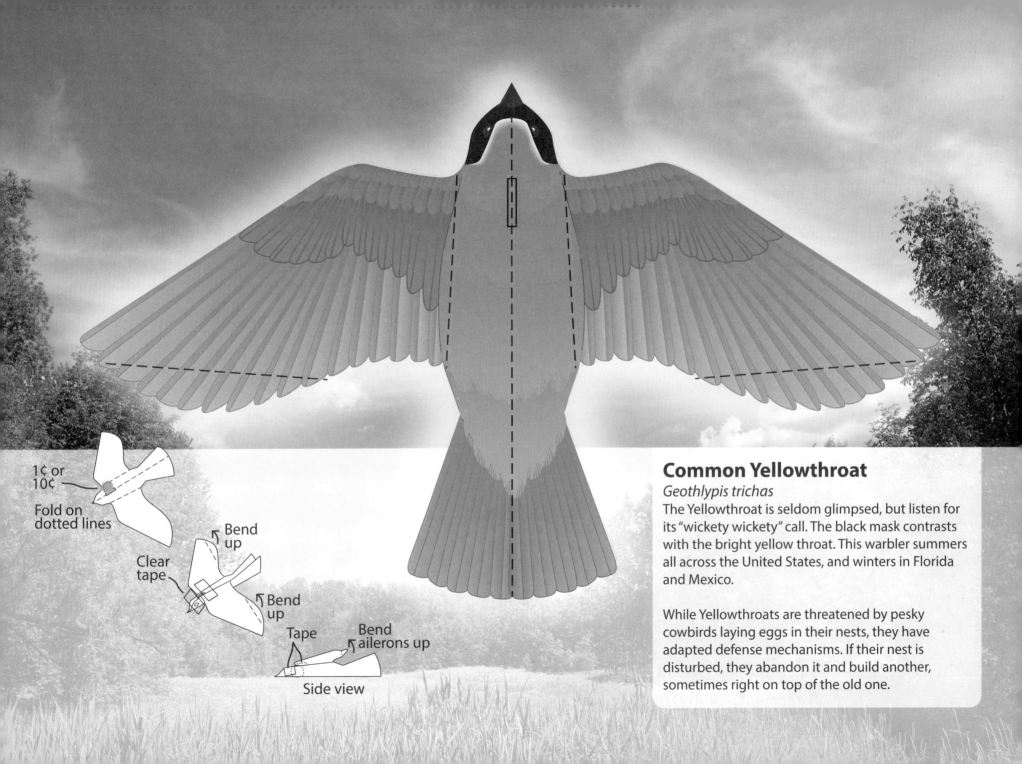

1¢ or 10¢

Fold on dotted lines

Clear tape

Bend up

Bend up

Tape

Bend ailerons up

Side view

Common Yellowthroat
Geothlypis trichas

The Yellowthroat is seldom glimpsed, but listen for its "wickety wickety" call. The black mask contrasts with the bright yellow throat. This warbler summers all across the United States, and winters in Florida and Mexico.

While Yellowthroats are threatened by pesky cowbirds laying eggs in their nests, they have adapted defense mechanisms. If their nest is disturbed, they abandon it and build another, sometimes right on top of the old one.

1¢ or 10¢

Fold on dotted lines

Clear tape

Bend up

Bend up

Tape

Bend ailerons up

Side view

Downy Woodpecker

Picoides pubescens

The Downy Woodpecker is the life of the party, whether in mixed forests, parks, or backyards. Patterned with black and white like a checkerboard, with a small red patch on males, it goes dip-dip-dip in flight. Its tail feathers have stiff points to brace it on the tree. Downies are common all across the United States.

Downy Woodpeckers nest in hollows in trees and peck for insects living under the bark. Their tiny bills can even find insect larvae inside the gall growths on goldenrod plants.

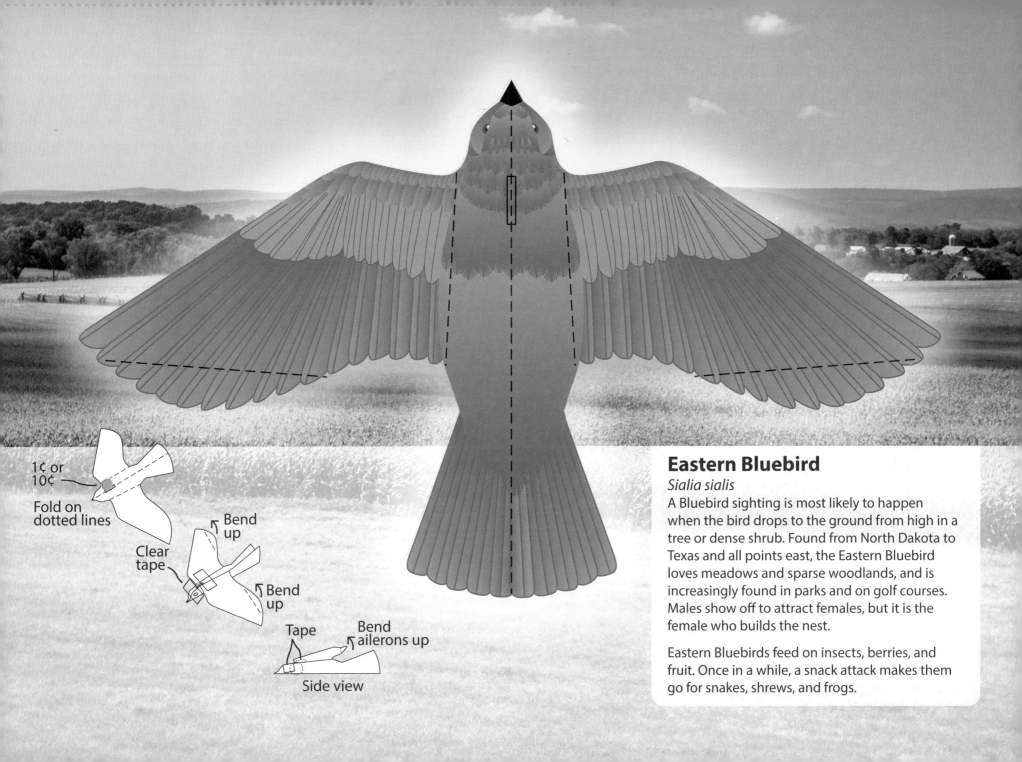

1¢ or 10¢

Fold on dotted lines

Clear tape

Bend up

Bend up

Tape

Bend ailerons up

Side view

Eastern Bluebird

Sialia sialis

A Bluebird sighting is most likely to happen when the bird drops to the ground from high in a tree or dense shrub. Found from North Dakota to Texas and all points east, the Eastern Bluebird loves meadows and sparse woodlands, and is increasingly found in parks and on golf courses. Males show off to attract females, but it is the female who builds the nest.

Eastern Bluebirds feed on insects, berries, and fruit. Once in a while, a snack attack makes them go for snakes, shrews, and frogs.

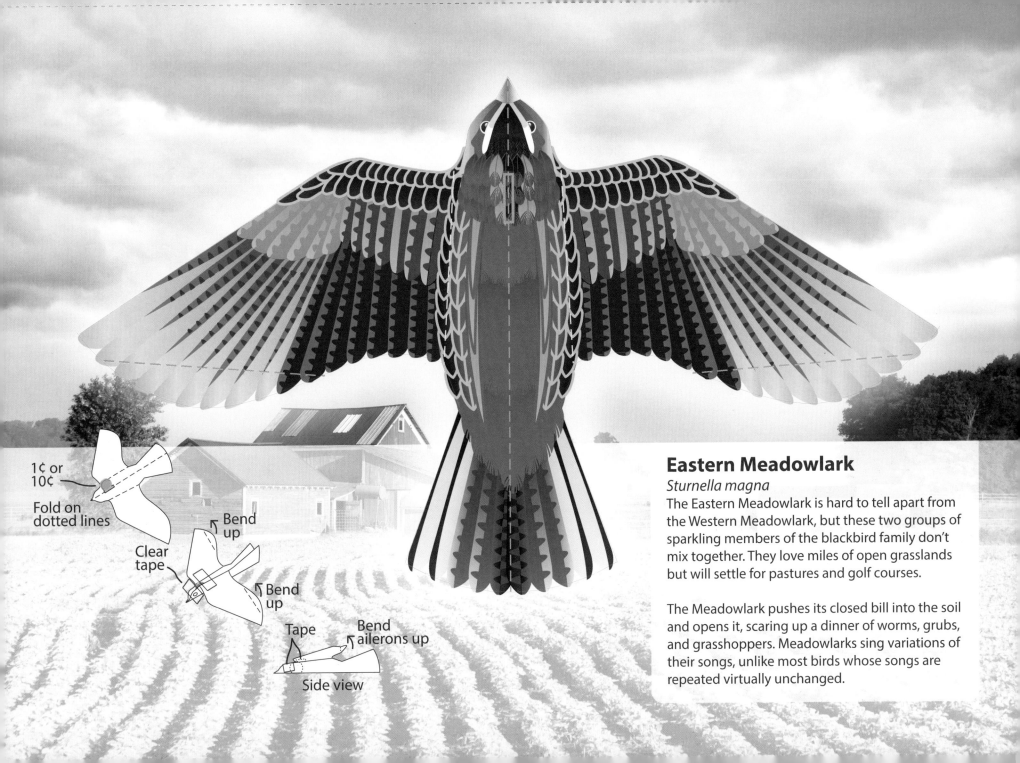

1¢ or 10¢

Fold on dotted lines

Clear tape

Bend up

Bend up

Tape

Bend ailerons up

Side view

Eastern Meadowlark

Sturnella magna

The Eastern Meadowlark is hard to tell apart from the Western Meadowlark, but these two groups of sparkling members of the blackbird family don't mix together. They love miles of open grasslands but will settle for pastures and golf courses.

The Meadowlark pushes its closed bill into the soil and opens it, scaring up a dinner of worms, grubs, and grasshoppers. Meadowlarks sing variations of their songs, unlike most birds whose songs are repeated virtually unchanged.

1¢ or 10¢

Fold on dotted lines

Clear tape

Bend up

Bend up

Tape

Bend ailerons up

Side view

Evening Grosbeak
Coccothraustes vespertinus

The brilliant contrast of the Evening Grosbeak's colors is visible in the northern forests it frequents, but you may find it throughout the United States. The Evening Grosbeak is omnivorous, eating insect larvae in warmer times, and feeding on seeds, berries, and fruits during colder months.

Evening Grosbeaks are found most often high in the branches of trees, though a flock of them can sometimes roam a neighborhood, hopping from feeder to feeder.

1¢ or
10¢

Fold on
dotted lines

Clear
tape

Bend
up

Bend
up

Tape

Bend
ailerons up

Side view

Golden-cheeked Warbler

Setophaga chrysoparia

This beautiful warbler is listed as an Endangered Species, for a good reason. It nests only in Central Texas, where cowbirds lay their eggs in its nest, threatening the warbler's young. Not only that, but its habitat is in danger from development, reducing the juniper (cedar) and scrub oak trees available for nesting.

Golden-cheeked Warblers eat insects they find while browsing in cedar and oak trees. They will sometimes hang upside down for tasty morsels!

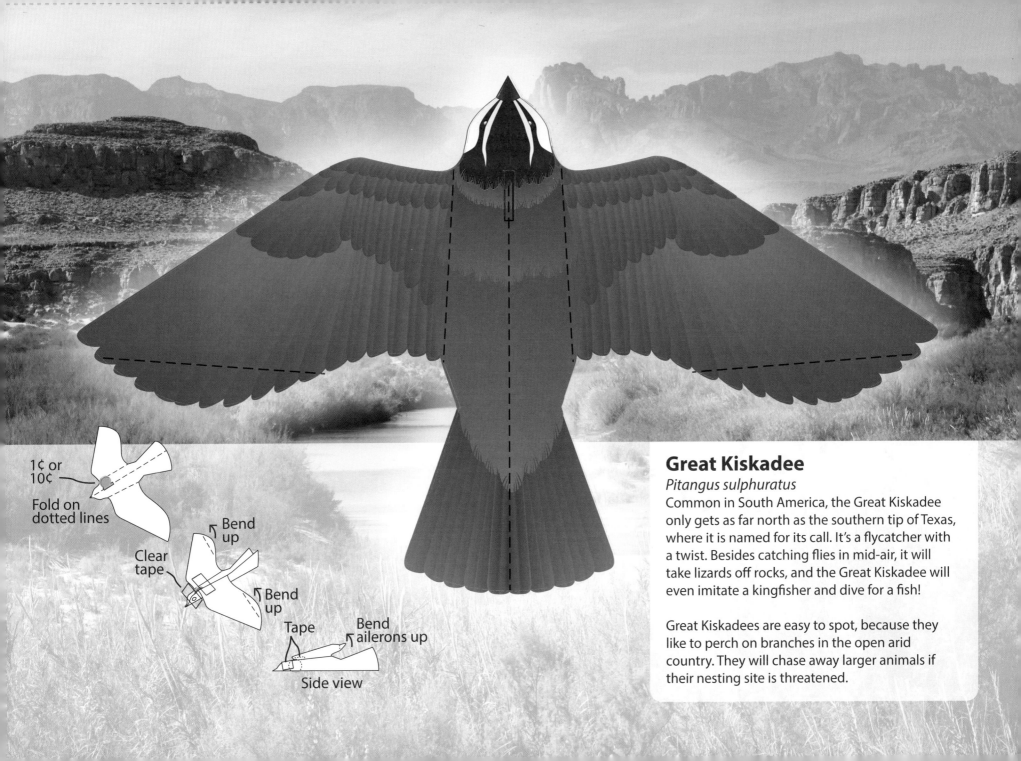

1¢ or 10¢

Fold on dotted lines

Bend up

Clear tape

Bend up

Tape

Bend ailerons up

Side view

Great Kiskadee

Pitangus sulphuratus

Common in South America, the Great Kiskadee only gets as far north as the southern tip of Texas, where it is named for its call. It's a flycatcher with a twist. Besides catching flies in mid-air, it will take lizards off rocks, and the Great Kiskadee will even imitate a kingfisher and dive for a fish!

Great Kiskadees are easy to spot, because they like to perch on branches in the open arid country. They will chase away larger animals if their nesting site is threatened.

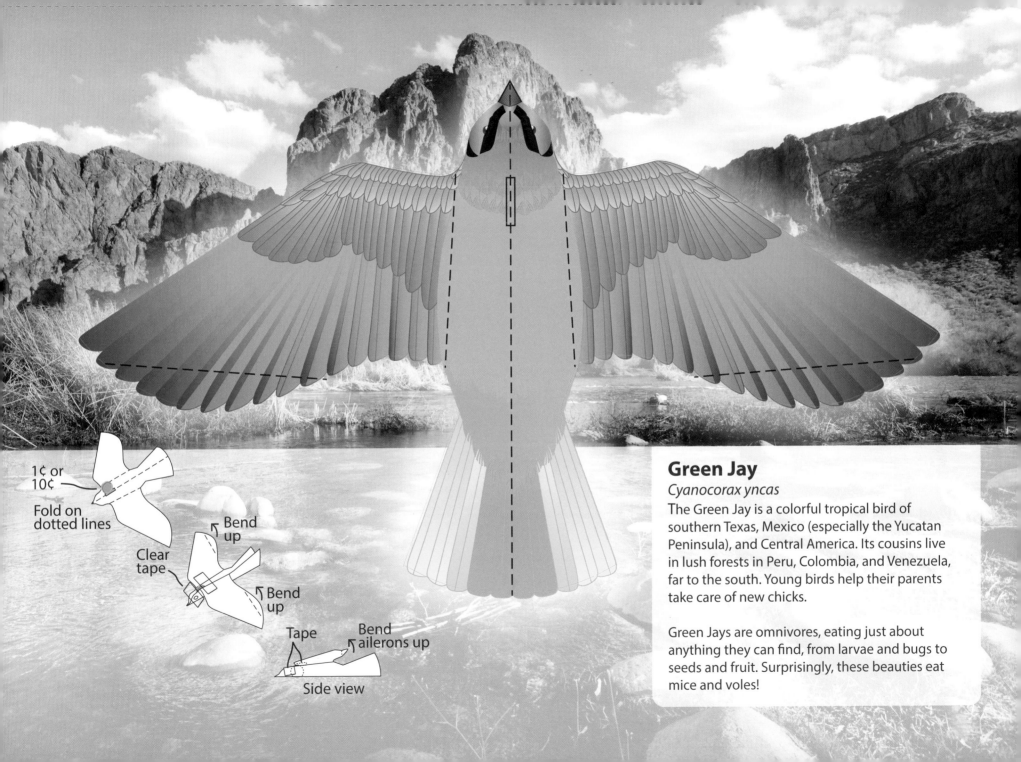

1¢ or 10¢

Fold on dotted lines

Clear tape

Bend up

Bend up

Tape

Bend ailerons up

Side view

Green Jay
Cyanocorax yncas

The Green Jay is a colorful tropical bird of southern Texas, Mexico (especially the Yucatan Peninsula), and Central America. Its cousins live in lush forests in Peru, Colombia, and Venezuela, far to the south. Young birds help their parents take care of new chicks.

Green Jays are omnivores, eating just about anything they can find, from larvae and bugs to seeds and fruit. Surprisingly, these beauties eat mice and voles!

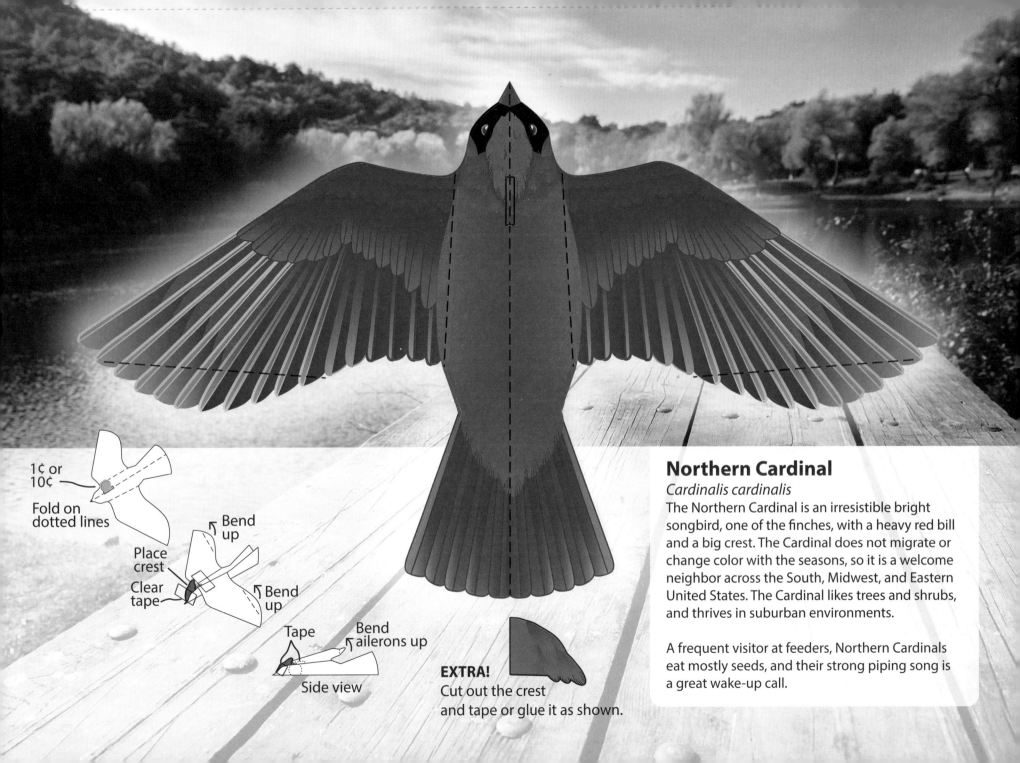

1¢ or 10¢

Fold on dotted lines

Place crest

Clear tape

Bend up

Bend up

Tape

Bend ailerons up

Side view

EXTRA!
Cut out the crest and tape or glue it as shown.

Northern Cardinal
Cardinalis cardinalis

The Northern Cardinal is an irresistible bright songbird, one of the finches, with a heavy red bill and a big crest. The Cardinal does not migrate or change color with the seasons, so it is a welcome neighbor across the South, Midwest, and Eastern United States. The Cardinal likes trees and shrubs, and thrives in suburban environments.

A frequent visitor at feeders, Northern Cardinals eat mostly seeds, and their strong piping song is a great wake-up call.

1¢ or
10¢

Fold on
dotted lines

Clear
tape

Bend
up

Bend
up

Tape

Bend
ailerons up

Side view

Painted Bunting

Passerina ciris

The Painted Bunting is a marvel of color, with a distinct tropical flavor. Summering in South Central United States, it winters in Mexico and Central America. This bird is shy, roosting and feeding in dense brush or tall grass, where it finds seeds to eat. The "near threatened" status of this bird kindles efforts to save it.

The truly fortunate may see Painted Buntings feeding in the open with a flock of Indigo Buntings while migrating: a magical sight!

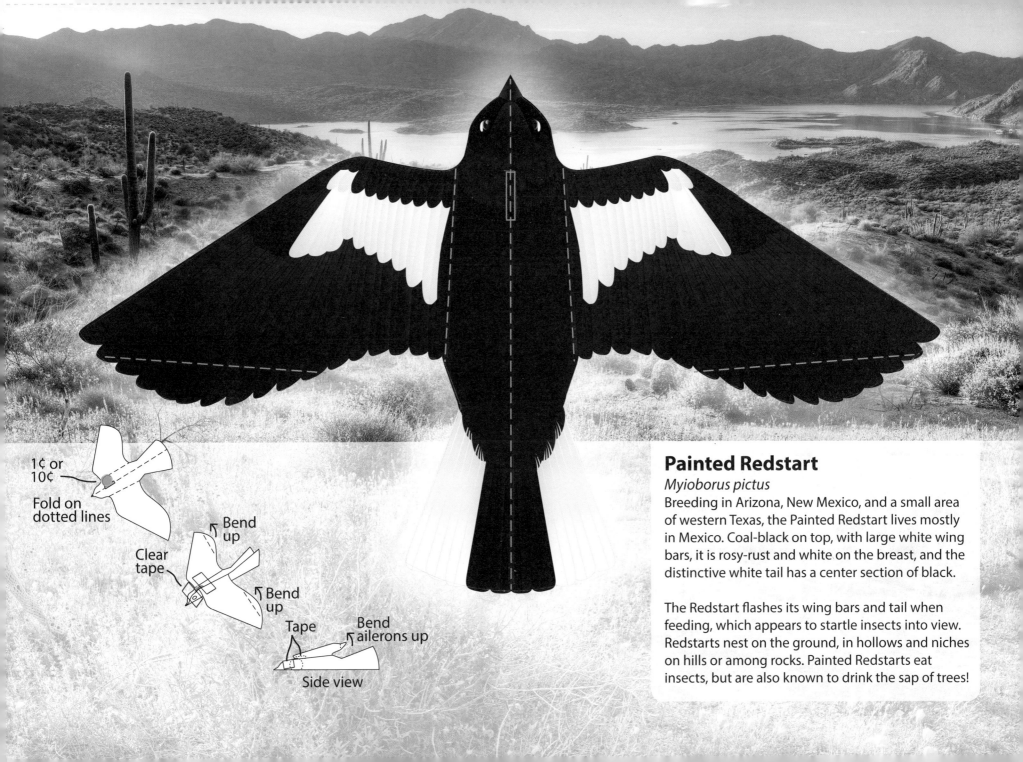

1¢ or 10¢

Fold on dotted lines

Clear tape

Bend up

Bend up

Tape

Bend ailerons up

Side view

Painted Redstart
Myioborus pictus

Breeding in Arizona, New Mexico, and a small area of western Texas, the Painted Redstart lives mostly in Mexico. Coal-black on top, with large white wing bars, it is rosy-rust and white on the breast, and the distinctive white tail has a center section of black.

The Redstart flashes its wing bars and tail when feeding, which appears to startle insects into view. Redstarts nest on the ground, in hollows and niches on hills or among rocks. Painted Redstarts eat insects, but are also known to drink the sap of trees!

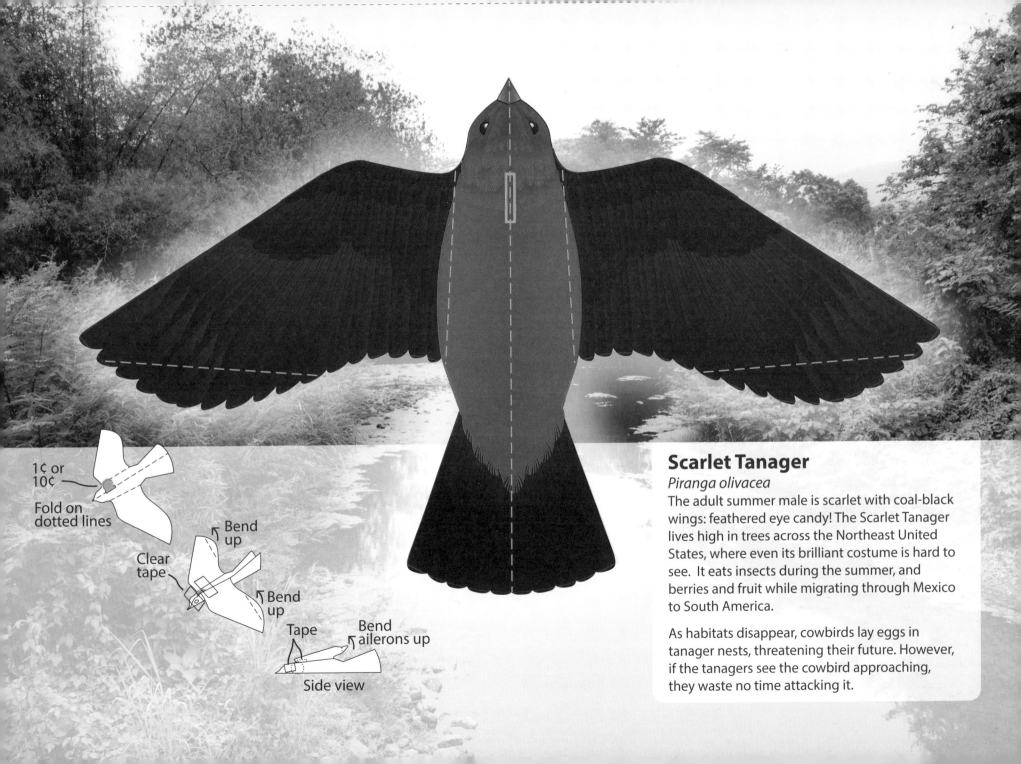

1¢ or 10¢

Fold on dotted lines

Clear tape

Bend up

Bend up

Tape

Bend ailerons up

Side view

Scarlet Tanager

Piranga olivacea

The adult summer male is scarlet with coal-black wings: feathered eye candy! The Scarlet Tanager lives high in trees across the Northeast United States, where even its brilliant costume is hard to see. It eats insects during the summer, and berries and fruit while migrating through Mexico to South America.

As habitats disappear, cowbirds lay eggs in tanager nests, threatening their future. However, if the tanagers see the cowbird approaching, they waste no time attacking it.

1¢ or
10¢

Fold on
dotted lines

Bend
up

Clear
tape

Bend
up

Tape

Bend
ailerons up

Side view

Varied Thrush

Ixoreus naevius

This member of the robin family is a reticent dweller of deep thickets and evergreen forests from northern California to Alaska. It likes water and feeds primarily on berries, either on the bush or after they've fallen. A backyard visitor on occasion, the Varied Thrush sometimes vacations in the East. Timber cutting may threaten its habitat.

The haunting call of the Varied Thrush is wistful and sad, emanating from the deep shadows of forest trees.

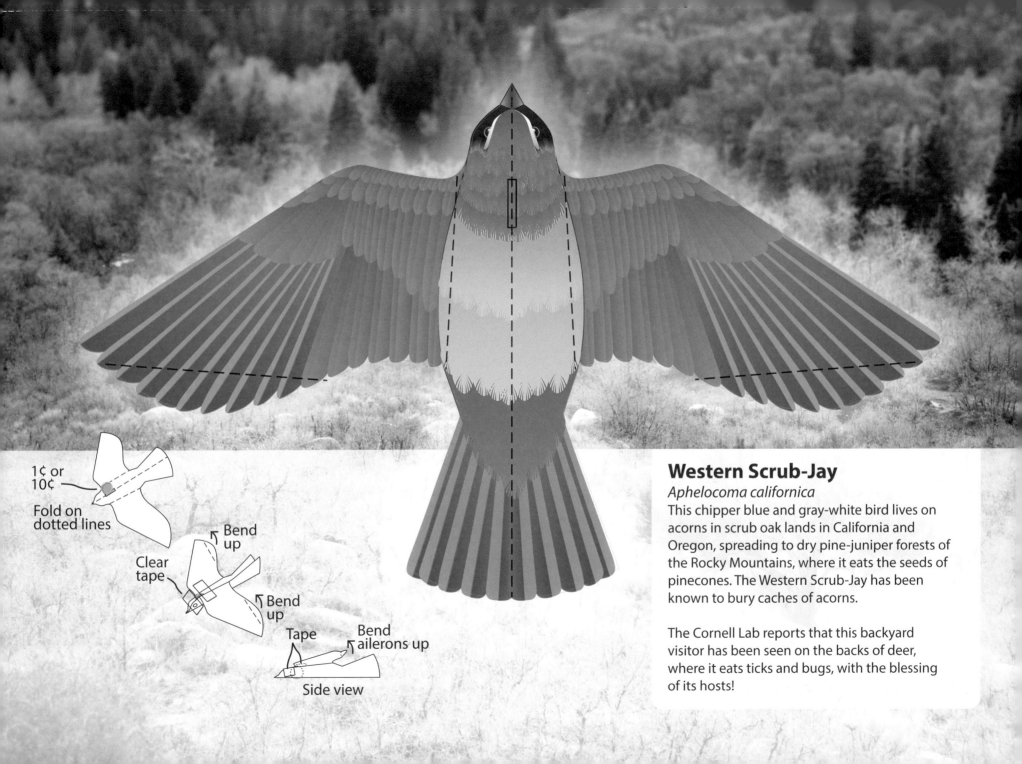

1¢ or
10¢

Fold on
dotted lines

Clear
tape

Bend
up

Bend
up

Tape

Bend
ailerons up

Side view

Western Scrub-Jay
Aphelocoma californica
This chipper blue and gray-white bird lives on acorns in scrub oak lands in California and Oregon, spreading to dry pine-juniper forests of the Rocky Mountains, where it eats the seeds of pinecones. The Western Scrub-Jay has been known to bury caches of acorns.

The Cornell Lab reports that this backyard visitor has been seen on the backs of deer, where it eats ticks and bugs, with the blessing of its hosts!

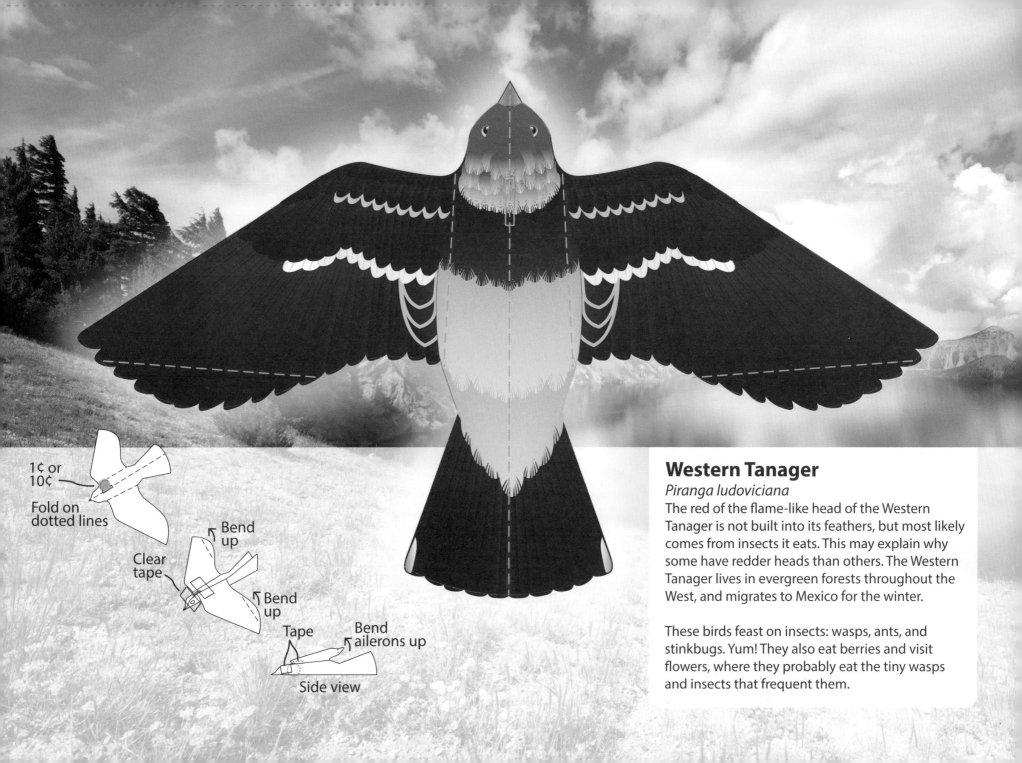

1¢ or 10¢

Fold on dotted lines

Clear tape

Bend up

Bend up

Bend ailerons up

Tape

Side view

Western Tanager

Piranga ludoviciana

The red of the flame-like head of the Western Tanager is not built into its feathers, but most likely comes from insects it eats. This may explain why some have redder heads than others. The Western Tanager lives in evergreen forests throughout the West, and migrates to Mexico for the winter.

These birds feast on insects: wasps, ants, and stinkbugs. Yum! They also eat berries and visit flowers, where they probably eat the tiny wasps and insects that frequent them.